MW01200741

YOU ARE THE DESIGNER OF YOUR OWN DESTINY

NAME: _____

"Optimism is the most important human trait, because it
allows us to evolve our ideas, to improve our situation, and to
hope for a better tomorrow." ~ Seth Godin

NEVER EVER
GIVE UP

"The best way to gain self-confidence is to do what you are afraid to do." – Unknown

MAKE IT
HAPPEN

think positive

"Happiness often sneaks in through a door
you didn't know you left open." – John
Barrymore

BELIEVE
YOU CAN

"When we are no longer able to change a situation, we are
challenged to change ourselves." – Viktor Frankl

BELIEVE IN
YOURSELF

"If you can change your mind, you can change your life." – William James

TAKE ACTION!

"When the world pushes you to your knees, you're in the perfect position to pray." – Rumi

NEVER EVER
GIVE UP

think positive

"The next time you feel slightly uncomfortable with the pressure in your life, remember no pressure, no diamonds. Pressure is a part of success." – Eric Thomas

MAKE IT HAPPEN

think positive

"You must make a decision that you are going to move on. It wont happen automatically. You will have to rise up and say, 'I don't care how hard this is, I don't care how disappointed I am, I'm not going to let this get the best of me. I'm moving on with my life." – Joel Osteen

BELIEVE
YOU CAN

think positive

"Be soft. Do not let the world make you hard. Do not let pain make you hate. Do not let the bitterness steal your sweetness. Take pride that even though the rest of the world may disagree, you still believe it to be a beautiful place." – Kurt Vonnegut

BELIEVE IN
YOURSELF

"Happiness, like unhappiness, is a proactive
choice." – Stephen Covey

TAKE ACTION!

think positive

"Success is falling nine times and getting up ten." – Jon Bon Jovi

NEVER EVER
GIVE UP

"All things are difficult before they are easy." – Thomas Fuller

MAKE IT
HAPPEN

"You are never too old to set another goal or dream a new dream." – C.S Lewis

BELIEVE
YOU CAN

"The difference in winning and losing is most often...not quitting." – Walt Disney

BELIEVE IN YOURSELF

think positive

"When I do good, I feel good. When I do bad, I feel bad. That's my religion." – Abraham Lincoln

TAKE ACTION!

"Whatever you want to do, do it now. There are only so many tomorrows." – Michael Landon

NEVER EVER
GIVE UP

think positive

"There is little difference in people, but that little difference makes a big difference. The little difference is attitude. The big difference is whether it is positive or negative." – W. Clement Stone

MAKE IT
HAPPEN

"If someone tells you, "You can't" they really mean, "I can't." – Sean Stephenson

BELIEVE
YOU CAN

think positive

"The difference between stumbling blocks and stepping stones is how you use them." – Unknown

BELIEVE IN YOURSELF

"We are responsible for what we are, and whatever we wish ourselves to be, we have the power to make ourselves." – Swami Vivekananda

TAKE ACTION!

"I am the greatest, I said that even before
I knew I was." – Muhammad Ali

NEVER EVER GIVE UP

think positive

"Take chances, make mistakes. That's how you grow. Pain nourishes your courage. You have to fail in order to practice being brave." – Mary Tyler Moore

MAKE IT HAPPEN

"If we're growing, we're always going to be out
of our comfort zone." – John C Maxwell

BELIEVE
YOU CAN

"The will to win, the desire to succeed, the urge to reach your full potential... these are the keys that will unlock the door to personal excellence." – Confucius

BELIEVE IN
YOURSELF

"All you can change is yourself, but sometimes that changes everything!" – Gary W Goldstein

TAKE ACTION!

"Success is not a destination but the consciousness of knowing that you are enjoying what you are doing and by doing it every day you are rewarded with great results." - Frank Mullani

NEVER EVER
GIVE UP

"No matter what the situation, remind yourself "I
have a choice." – Deepak Chopra

MAKE IT
HAPPEN

"If you think you can do a thing or think you can't do a thing, you're right." – Henry Ford

BELIEVE
YOU CAN

"We are all here for some special reason. Stop being a prisoner of your past. Become the architect of your future." – Robin Sharma

BELIEVE IN
YOURSELF

think positive

"Life is a gift, and it offers us the privilege, opportunity, and responsibility to give something back by becoming more." – Tony Robbins

TAKE ACTION!

"Today is a new beginning, a chance to turn your failures into achievements & your sorrows into so goods. No room for excuses."
— Joel Brown

NEVER EVER
GIVE UP

"If you want light to come into your life, you
need to stand where it is shining." – Guy Finley

MAKE IT
HAPPEN

"Happiness is an attitude. We either make ourselves miserable, or happy and strong. The amount of work is the same." – Francesca Reigler

BELIEVE
YOU CAN

"Hope is a waking dream." – Aristotle

BELIEVE IN YOURSELF

"You yourself, as much as anybody in the entire
universe, deserve your love and affection." – Buddha

TAKE
ACTION!

"I've had a lot of worries in my life, most of which never happened" – Mark Twain

NEVER EVER
GIVE UP

"Learning is a gift. Even when pain is your
teacher." – Maya Watson

MAKE IT HAPPEN

"I may not have gone where I intended to go, but I think I have ended up where I needed to be." – Douglas Adams

BELIEVE
YOU CAN

"Our greatest weakness lies in giving up. The most certain way to succeed is always to try just one more time." – Thomas Edison

BELIEVE IN YOURSELF

"We don't see things as they are, we see them
as we are." – Anaís Nin

TAKE ACTION!

"The only place where your dream becomes impossible is in your own thinking." – Robert H Schuller

NEVER EVER
GIVE UP

"If you can dream it, then you can achieve it. You will get all you want in life if you help enough other people get what they want." – Zig Ziglar

MAKE IT HAPPEN

"Success consists of going from failure to failure
without loss of enthusiasm." – Winston Churchill

BELIEVE
YOU CAN

"An attitude of positive expectation is the mark of
the superior personality." – Brian Tracy

BELIEVE IN
YOURSELF

think positive

"If opportunity doesn't knock, build a door." – Milton Berle

TAKE
ACTION!

"Believe in yourself! Have faith in your abilities! Without a humble but reasonable confidence in your own powers you cannot be successful or happy." – Norman Vincent Peale

NEVER EVER
GIVE UP

"The way to get started is to quit talking and begin doing." - Walt Disney

MAKE IT
HAPPEN

"Happiness is not something readymade. It comes from your own actions." - Dalai Lama

BELIEVE
YOU CAN

"Challenges are what make life interesting and overcoming them is what makes life meaningful." - *Joshua J. Marine*

BELIEVE IN YOURSELF

"It is never too late to be what you might have been." - George Eliot

TAKE ACTION!

"Life is what we make it, always has been,
always will be." - Grandma Moses

NEVER EVER
GIVE UP

"I am thankful for all of those who said NO to me. Its because of them I'm doing it myself. " - Albert Einstein

MAKE IT
HAPPEN

think
positive

"Do what makes YOU happy." - Malcolm Matthews

BELIEVE
YOU CAN

"The mind is everything. What you think
you become." - Buddha

BELIEVE IN
YOURSELF

BELIEVE IN
YOURSELF

TAKE
ACTION!

NEVER EVER
GIVE UP

MAKE IT
HAPPEN

CREATIVE JOURNALS FACTORY

THANK YOU WE HOPE YOU LIKE YOUR NOTEBOOK - JOURNAL
PLEASE WRITE YOUR REVIEW, IT MEANS A LOT TO US!

FIND MORE AMAZING JOURNALS, DIARIES & NOTEBOOKS AT:
www.CreativeJournalsFactory.com

Made in the USA
Coppell, TX
16 April 2022

76613558R00070